GIFTS to MAKE with

Crayola M

MODEL MAGIC®

KIM FERNANDES

Scholastic Canada Ltd.

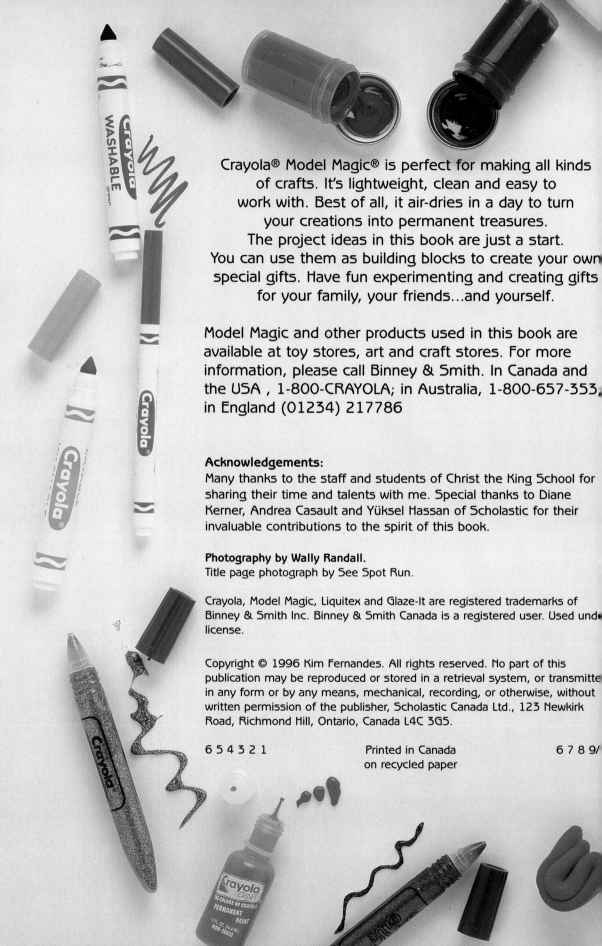

Crayola® Model Magic® is perfect for making all kinds of crafts. It's lightweight, clean and easy to work with. Best of all, it air-dries in a day to turn your creations into permanent treasures. The project ideas in this book are just a start. You can use them as building blocks to create your own special gifts. Have fun experimenting and creating gifts for your family, your friends...and yourself.

Model Magic and other products used in this book are available at toy stores, art and craft stores. For more information, please call Binney & Smith. In Canada and the USA , 1-800-CRAYOLA; in Australia, 1-800-657-353, in England (01234) 217786

Acknowledgements:
Many thanks to the staff and students of Christ the King School for sharing their time and talents with me. Special thanks to Diane Kerner, Andrea Casault and Yüksel Hassan of Scholastic for their invaluable contributions to the spirit of this book.

Photography by Wally Randall.
Title page photograph by See Spot Run.

6 5 4 3 2 1   Printed in Canada   6 7 8 9/
                     on recycled paper

⇨ Make sure your hands and work surface are clean and dry.

⇨ Work on a cookie sheet, or cover your work surface with plastic to keep your projects from sticking.

⇨ If the Model Magic is too sticky when you first open the package, just roll it in your hands for a few minutes until it becomes firmer.

⇨ Model Magic dries fast. Take out only as much as you need and roll the rest back up in the foil pouch to squeeze the air out. Store the pouch in an air-tight container.

⇨ Fresh, wet Model Magic bonds perfectly to dry pieces, so you can build your projects in stages. There's no need to rush!

⇨ Model Magic air-dries in about 24 hours. DO NOT try to dry it in an oven.

⇨ To help your creations dry evenly, turn them over after a few hours.

⇨ Thick pieces of Model Magic can take a long time to dry completely. When making large items, try building over a base of aluminum foil, plastic foam or cardboard.

⇨ Some of these projects use pins and knives; you might want to get help from an adult for these crafts.

TOOLS AND TECHNIQUES

Shapes

Make snakes and balls by rolling Model Magic between your hands. Try using cookie cutters to stamp out crisp, flat shapes.

Tools

A plastic knife is great for cutting wet Model Magic. Scissors work on wet or dry Model Magic — try pinking shears on dry pieces for a jagged edge. Use a toothpick to add details. A drinking glass can be used as a rolling pin to flatten out pieces.

Marbling

For a marbled effect, make snakes using two or more colors. Twist them together and roll into a snake again. Bend in half, twist and roll again until you get the look you want.

Glue

You can add sequins, rhinestones, wiggly eyes and other objects to dried creations with Crayola Fabric & Craft Paint® or white glue. Crayola Glaze-It® or white glue are also good for gluing together broken pieces.

Textures

Press different objects — keys, forks, leaves, and more — into damp Model Magic to add texture.

Finishing

Dry material can be smoothed with fine sandpaper or an emery board.
Pieces that will be handled a lot or that might get damp should be glazed to protect them — try Crayola Glaze-It.

Paint and Markers

Make sure your creation is completely dry before using paint or markers. Acrylic paints work best. Crayola Fabric & Craft Paint and Liquitex® Acrylic Paint are recommended.
For a raised effect, squeeze fabric paint or glitter glue directly onto your creation. Marker ink may "bleed" into the surface — experiment to get different looks.

Mixing Colours

You can blend existing colours of Model Magic to make new shades. As in marbling, make snakes, twist and roll; keep mixing until you have one even colour. A mixing chart is shown below. For pastels, start with white and mix a little bit of a colour in.

★ = ★ + ★ ★

★ = ★ + ★ ★ ★ ★

★ = ★ ★ ★ + ★ ★

★ = ★ ★ + ★ ★ ★

★ = ★ ★ ★ ★ + ★

★ = ★ ★ ★ ★ ★ + ★

★ = ★ ★ ★ ★ ★ ★ ★ ★ + ★

★ = ★ ★ ★ ★ ★ ★ ★ ★ ★ ★ + ★ ★ + ★

★ = ★ ★ ★ ★ ★ ★ ★ ★ ★ ★ + ★ ★ + ★

★ = ★ ★ ★ ★ ★ ★ ★ ★ ★ ★ + ★

5

SIMPLE JEWELRY

It would be easy to fill a whole book with jewelry ideas. Here are just a few simple projects to get you started. Try them out, then design your own special jewelry gifts.

Basic Beads

Materials

✔ Model Magic
✔ scissors
✔ pin
✔ embroidery thread or dental floss
✔ a piece of wire
✔ glaze and brush
✔ jewelry clasps (optional)

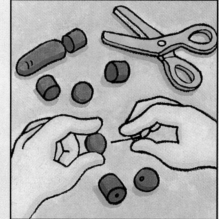

Plain beads

You can make these with solid colors or a marbled mixture.

■ Roll Model Magic into an even snake shape.

■ Use scissors to cut the snake into pieces.

■ Roll the pieces between your hands to make balls, or shape them into cylinders, ovals or squares.

■ To make holes for stringing, hold a bead gently between your fingers. Slowly push the pin halfway through the bead, turning the pin gently and wiggling it to make the hole larger.

■ Turn the bead around and do the same to the other side until the two holes join up.

■ Let dry, then glaze

Wrap beads

■ Roll a small snake and taper the ends.

■ Wrap the snake around a

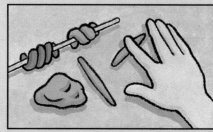

piece of wire to make a spiral shape.

■ Let dry, then glaze.

■ Pull the wire out to release the bead.

Making a beaded necklace or bracelet

■ Cut a piece of embroidery thread or dental floss long enough to go around your wrist or neck. Don't forget to leave extra at the ends for knotting.

■ String the beads on to the thread.

■ Tie on jewelry clasps or knot the ends of the thread to finish your piece.

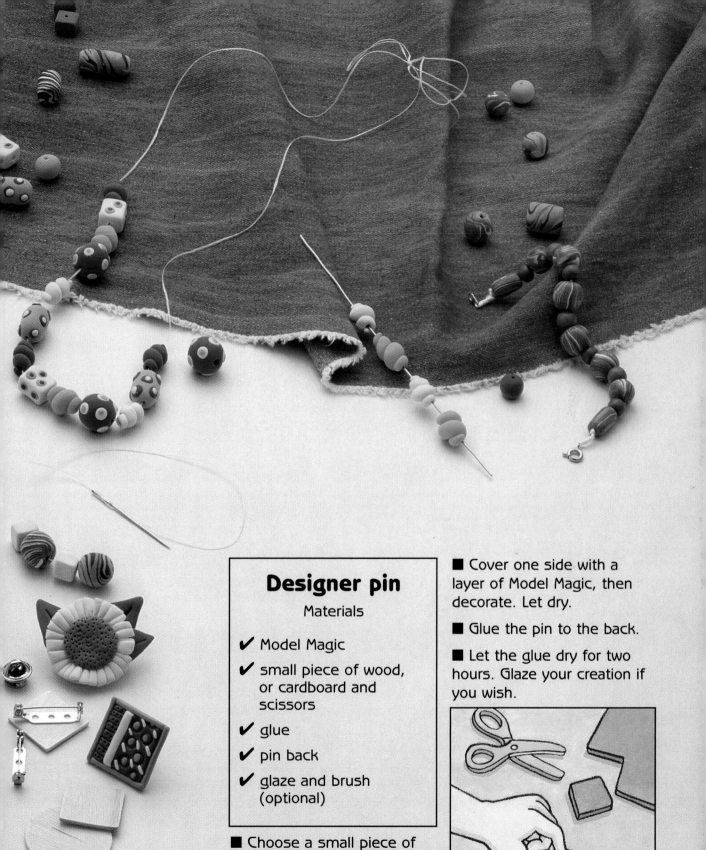

Designer pin

Materials

✔ Model Magic
✔ small piece of wood, or cardboard and scissors
✔ glue
✔ pin back
✔ glaze and brush (optional)

■ Choose a small piece of wood, or cut a piece of cardboard about 11/2" (4 cm) square.

■ Cover one side with a layer of Model Magic, then decorate. Let dry.

■ Glue the pin to the back.

■ Let the glue dry for two hours. Glaze your creation if you wish.

Big Bangle

Materials

- ✔ Model Magic
- ✔ scissors
- ✔ tape
- ✔ cardboard
- ✔ ruler
- ✔ rhinestones (optional)
- ✔ glaze and brush

■ Cut a piece of cardboard about 10" (25 cm) long. Wrap it loosely around your wrist, so that you can easily

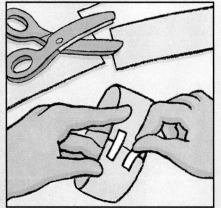

slide it on and off, even with a layer of Model Magic on it. Use tape to secure the loop.

■ Roll out a thick snake of Model Magic, flatten it, then wrap it around the cardboard loop. Alternate two or more

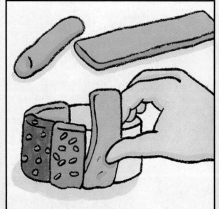

colors, if you like, until the loop is completely covered.

■ Decorate your bangle with shapes, or press in rhinestones.

■ Let dry, then glaze.

Twisty Earrings

Materials

✔ Model Magic
✔ scissors
✔ cardboard
✔ glue
✔ earring clips or posts
✔ glaze and brush

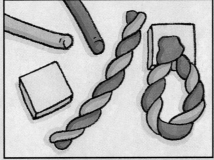

■ Cut two small, identical shapes from cardboard to make the base of each earring.

■ Choose two colors of Model Magic. Roll them into snakes of equal length, then twist them together. Cut twist in half with scissors.

■ Bend each half into a loop, and press a loop to the front of each earring base.

■ Cover the front and back of each base with one of the two twist colors. Add a small dot of the second color to the front. Let dry.

■ Glue an earring clip or post to the back of each base and let dry for two hours.

■ Glaze the front and back of the earrings, letting one side dry completely before glazing the other side.

9

MAGNETS

Fish are just a start — you can make all sorts of beautiful and useful magnets. Try creating animals, monsters, or your favorite foods!

Funny Fish

Materials

✔ Model Magic
✔ scissors
✔ glue
✔ magnet
✔ wiggly eyes (optional)
✔ glaze and brush (optional)

■ Make an oval shape and flatten it to create the body.

■ Use scissors to cut out a mouth. Attach a triangle for the tail, and mold it with your

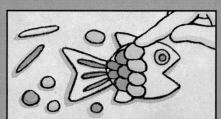

fingers or cut a notch from the end. Add two smaller triangles for fins.

■ Make an eye by layering two or three dots of different colors, or add a wiggly eye. If you want to add scales, overlap flattened circles, starting from the back of the fish.

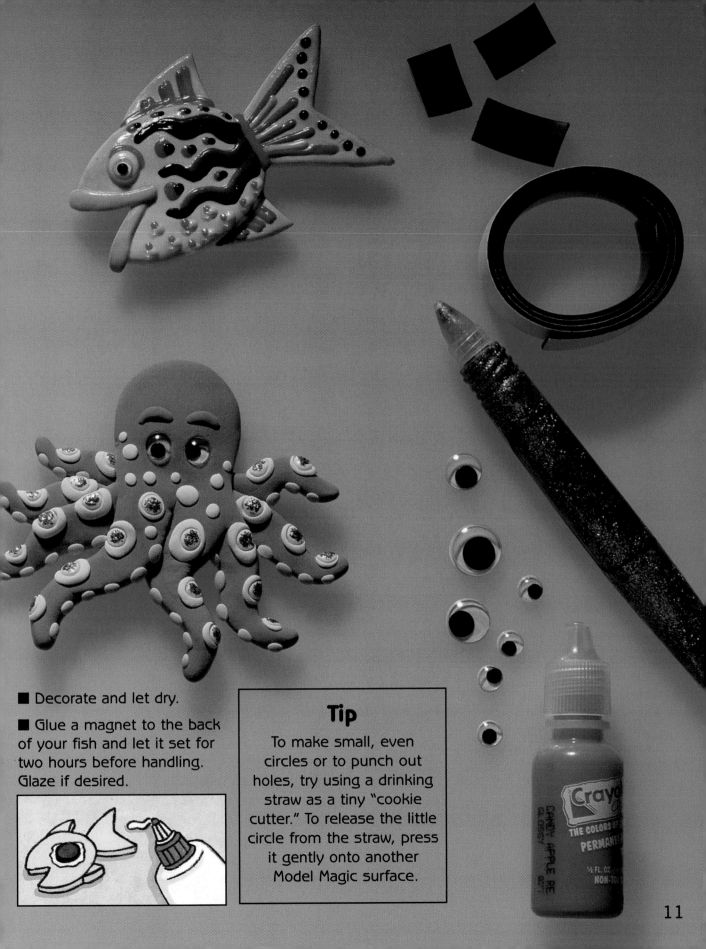

■ Decorate and let dry.

■ Glue a magnet to the back of your fish and let it set for two hours before handling. Glaze if desired.

Tip

To make small, even circles or to punch out holes, try using a drinking straw as a tiny "cookie cutter." To release the little circle from the straw, press it gently onto another Model Magic surface.

FINGER PUPPETS

Try creating a miniature replica of your pet, or make the animal you've always wanted — a bunny, a cat or maybe a dragon! You can create a whole zoo to fit on your fingers.

■ Cut a slit up the side of your cardboard tube, then cut a ring about the length of your finger. Gently squeeze the ring to fit around your finger and tape the sides together.

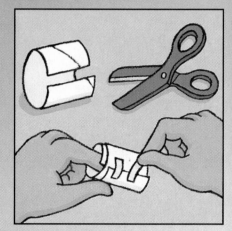

Bunny Puppet Pet
Materials

- ✔ Model Magic
- ✔ cardboard tube
- ✔ scissors
- ✔ tape
- ✔ aluminum foil
- ✔ fishing line (optional)
- ✔ glaze and brush (optional)

■ Crumple foil into a ball to form a head. Tape it to the top of your tube. Now you're ready to build your puppet.

■ Cover the ball and tube with Model Magic and press it into shape.

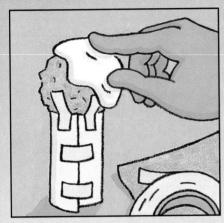

■ To make the bunny's head, add two dots for eyes and a small triangle for the nose. Push in small pieces of fishing line for whiskers.

■ Roll out two small snakes, flatten them, and attach them to the top of the head for ears.

■ Roll out two snakes for arms and attach to the sides of the body. If you like, make a carrot for the bunny to hold.

■ Stick a ball onto the back for a tail. Let dry.

Tip

Try making your animal on the end of a pencil, instead, to create a fancy pencil-topper!

Wizard puppet by Kenny Lee.

PICTURE FRAMES

A frame makes a wonderful gift, especially if you put a memorable photo in it. The fancy frame takes a little extra work to construct but the results are worth it. You may need an adult to help you with the cutting.

Simple Frame

Materials

- ✔ Model Magic
- ✔ photograph
- ✔ pencil
- ✔ cardboard
- ✔ tape
- ✔ two large paper clips
- ✔ scissors
- ✔ cookie cutters (optional)

■ Cut a piece of cardboard a bit bigger than your photograph. Center the photo on the board and tape it down.

■ Cover the exposed cardboard with Model Magic to

make a border. Overlap the edges of the photo and wrap the Model Magic around the outside edges of the frame. Decorate and let dry.

■ To make the stand, take two large paper clips and bend them open to make an L shape. Attach the small sides to the back of the cardboard with wads of Model Magic. Let dry.

Fancy Frame

Materials

- ✔ photograph
- ✔ ruler
- ✔ pencil
- ✔ heavy cardboard or illustration board
- ✔ art knife
- ✔ glue

■ Cut out three identical pieces of board, about 6"x 8" (15 cm x 20 cm) each. Set one aside for the backing. Cut a strip about 2" x 6" (5 cm x 15 cm) for the stand, and score it (cut partway through) an inch (2.5 cm) from the end to make a tab.

■ Place a photograph in the center of the second board and trace around it with a pencil. Use the art knife to cut just **outside** the outline. Then cut the middle piece away from the top edge to create a U-shape into which your picture will slide.

■ Trace the same photograph outline on the third board and cut just

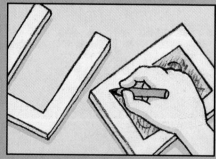

inside the lines to make the front of the frame.

■ Cover the front piece with Model Magic and decorate it with shapes, or press in objects to get interesting textures. Let dry.

■ To assemble, glue the U-shaped board to the plain backing. Then glue the Model Magic frame to the U-shape. Attach the stand by gluing the top of the tab to the back. Let dry for one hour, then slide in your photo.

DECORATED BOXES

Here's a simple way to create a beautiful keepsake. You can make the floral box shown, but there are lots of other possibilities. Try pressing shells, pebbles or buttons into the lid. Or you can add paint, textures or cut-out shapes to make your box unique.

Floral Box

Materials

✔ Model Magic

✔ small gift box with removable lid

✔ dried or silk flowers and leaves

✔ glaze and brush

✔ paint (optional)

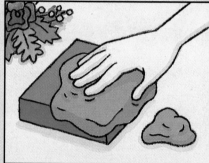

■ Cover the outside of the lid with Model Magic.

■ Gently press your flowers and leaves into the lid. Make a long, thin snake and wrap it around the bottom edge of the lid to create a border. Let dry.

■ Remove the lid from the box and set the bottom aside. Cut the stems off the flowers. If you like, you can arrange them on the lid until you're pleased with the design, then remove your arrangement.

■ Glaze twice, letting each coat dry at least two hours. Paint the box bottom, if you wish.

16

PAPER CLIP CREATURES

This fun and easy project requires only Model Magic, a paper clip and your imagination. You can make lizards, snakes and bugs to hang from a collar, a shirt pocket, the outside of a glass or a flower pot!

Lazy Lizard
Materials

✔ Model Magic
✔ large paper clip
✔ toothpick
✔ glaze and brush (optional)

■ Create the body of the lizard by rolling out a snake of Model Magic that is thick on one end and thin on the other. Flatten it slightly and curve the thin end to make a tail. Make an oval shape for the head and attach to the body.

  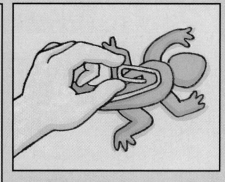

■ To make the legs, roll out four snakes and attach to the sides of the body. Bend the hind legs back and the front legs forward. Use the toothpick to carve toes.

■ Add small circles for the eyes and use the toothpick to poke two holes for the nose. Decorate your lizard with Model Magic patterns, or wait until it dries and use markers or paint.

■ Get a large paper clip and pry it open so that it fits over your shirt collar or pocket. Gently press the large side of the paper clip into the back of your lizard until it is completely embedded. Let dry. Glaze your creature if you wish.

(If the paper clip comes off, just glue it back on.)

BOUQUET OF FLOWERS

Unlike real flowers, your Model Magic roses won't wilt. You can make a single rose or a whole bouquet tied together with an attractive ribbon. Display your flowers in a drinking glass or a small vase.

Everlasting Roses

Materials

- ✔ Model Magic
- ✔ green pipe cleaners
- ✔ scissors
- ✔ glue
- ✔ toothpick
- ✔ drinking glass or jar

■ Cut a pipe cleaner into stems about 6" (15 cm) long. Make Model Magic leaves by flattening a green ball, then pinching one end. Run a toothpick down the middle to draw on a vein. Set leaves aside to dry.

■ To make a rose, roll out a snake of Model Magic about 2" (5 cm) long and flatten it.

Wrap it around the top of your stem, pinching it at the bottom. Make petals from flattened ovals and place them around the center until the flower looks full. Don't make your rose too big or the stem will bend.

■ Stand roses in a drinking glass to dry. Don't let them touch each other before they dry, or they will stick together. Glue leaves to the stems of your finished roses and let dry another hour before displaying.

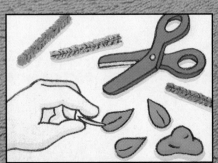

Tip

Need a fancy vase to hold your bouquet? Create one yourself by making a basic Pencil Holder (see page 25) and decorating it to match your blooms.

Flowers behind the fence by Angel Lo.

MOBILES

Create a collection of Model Magic objects to spin and turn from a mobile. Try making a flock of birds, or use cookie cutters to make bright and easy shapes.

Bird Mobile

Materials

- ✔ Model Magic
- ✔ pencil and ruler
- ✔ corrugated cardboard
- ✔ scissors or art knife
- ✔ 8 small paper clips
- ✔ pin
- ✔ paint and brush
- ✔ string, fishing line or dental floss
- ✔ 8 small plastic-foam balls

■ Cut a piece of cardboard about 6" (15 cm) square. Poke a hole near each corner using a pin. Make four more holes, one halfway along each side. Paint the piece of cardboard and let dry.

■ Cut eight pieces of string about a yard (1 m) long. Make a large knot in the middle of each piece, then thread one through each of the holes in the cardboard. Collect all the strings at the top, making sure the cardboard is hanging straight, and tie them into one big knot.

■ Make each bird by pushing a paper clip into a foam ball, leaving a loop exposed at the top. Cover with Model Magic to form the body. Make triangle shapes for the tail and wings and attach.

■ Make a smaller ball of Model Magic for the head. Attach it to the body, adding dots for eyes and a triangle for a beak. Decorate and let dry.

■ Tie a finished bird to the end of each string. Cut some strings shorter than others so the birds will hang at different levels.

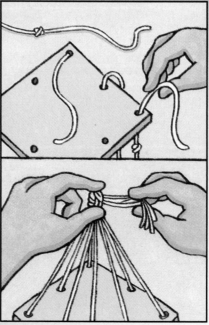

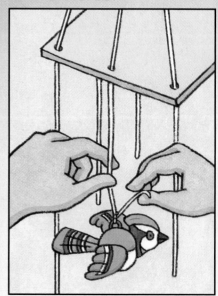

DESK ORGANIZERS

Here are two simple projects that will help brighten up a desk and keep it neat. When looking for a stone to make your paperweight, choose one with a flat bottom. Let the shape of your stone help determine what you create.

Cat Paperweight

Materials

✔ Model Magic
✔ stone
✔ toothpick
✔ paint and brush (optional)

■ Find a stone about the size of a large egg. Rinse it clean, and dry.

■ Cover stone completely with Model Magic to form the body. Make two oval shapes with paws for the back legs and attach to the body. Roll out two snakes for the front legs and a long thin one for the tail, and attach. Carve out toes with the toothpick.

■ Roll a ball of Model Magic for the head, and join it to the front. Add two triangle shapes for ears, two small circles for eyes, and a

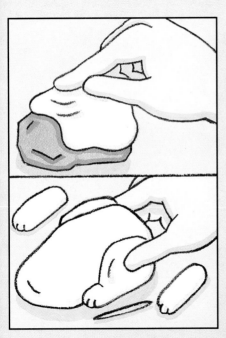

smaller triangle for the nose.

■ Use a toothpick to draw on a mouth, and poke whisker holes around the nose. Let dry, then paint on stripes or spots, if you like.

Pencil Holder

Materials

✔ Model Magic

✔ empty juice can

✔ paper clips, staples, etc. to decorate (optional)

■ Rinse out the can. Flatten a sheet of Model Magic and wrap it around the can, smoothing it out until the outside is completely covered.

■ Decorate your container with Model Magic shapes, or try embedding desk objects like paper clips, staples and short pencils into the sides. Let dry. If the objects come off, glue them on firmly.

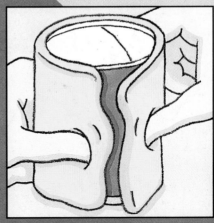

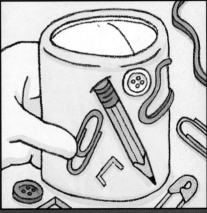

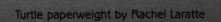

Turtle paperweight by Rachel Laratte

MOVABLE CARS

These cars don't just look good — they're fun to wheel around. With a little imagination and some photographs to guide you, you can make cars, buses or trucks.

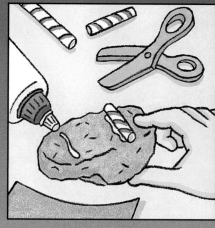

Sports Car

Materials

- ✔ Model Magic
- ✔ aluminum foil
- ✔ drinking straw
- ✔ scissors
- ✔ glue or tape
- ✔ round toothpicks
- ✔ ruler

■ Cut two pieces of straw about 1/2" (1 cm) shorter than the toothpicks. Then crumple a sheet of foil to make a base for your car shape. Make sure the car is no wider than the length of the straws.

■ Glue or tape the straws to the bottom of the car, about 1 1/2" (4 cm) apart. If you are using glue, let it dry for two hours.

■ Cover the foil base with Model Magic. Press out a

sheet to cover the bottom of the car and another for the top, then mold them together and shape your car. (Make sure not to cover the ends of the straws!) Decorate and set aside to dry.

■ Roll out four equal-sized balls for the wheels and flatten them to about 1/4"

(.5 cm) thick. Let your car and wheels dry for a couple of hours.

■ To attach the wheels, put toothpicks through the straws. Push the wheels onto the toothpicks. Roll your car to see if it runs smoothly and adjust the wheels if necessary.

■ To secure your wheels, make some hubcaps. Roll out four smaller balls of Model Magic and press one onto the center of each wheel, covering the ends of the toothpicks. Now your car is done — leave it overnight

to dry completely, then you're ready to roll!

MASKS

A mask can be fun to use as a disguise for a party or Halloween. It also makes a wonderful gift that can be hung up on a wall.

Monster Mask

Materials

- ✔ Model Magic
- ✔ plastic knife
- ✔ glue
- ✔ popsicle stick, tongue depressor or other stick for a handle
- ✔ picture hanger (optional)

■ Flatten a large piece of Model Magic to about 1/4" (.5 cm) thick. Make it wide enough to fit in front of your face. Use the plastic knife to cut it into the shape you want.

■ Cut eye holes out of your mask while it is still damp. Make sure they are big enough so that you can see out easily.

■ Decorate your monster mask with more Model Magic or press in feathers and other objects. Or wait until the mask is dry and use paint and markers to make your designs.

■ When the mask is dry, glue the stick to the bottom corner or glue a hanger to the back to mount your mask on a wall. Let the glue dry for at least two hours before picking the mask up or hanging it.

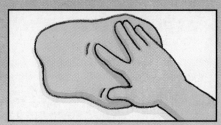

Tip

Try using cookie cutters to make crisp, clean eye holes for your mask. You don't have to use round ones — try picking an interesting shape instead!

28

3-D PICTURES

Use your imagination to create a picture of your back yard — or try making a portrait of yourself, your family or your friends.

Landscape

Materials

✔ Model Magic
✔ scrap piece of wood, or cardboard and scissors
✔ picture hanger
✔ glue
✔ paint and brush (optional)

■ Use a scrap of wood or cut out a piece of cardboard for your base. To create a landscape, start with the sky. Use paint, or flatten a large piece of Model Magic onto the top half of your base and spread it out with your fingers. Leave a small border all around.

■ Use paint or Model Magic to make the ground. Spread the Model Magic out, letting it overlap the bottom edge of the sky.

■ Fill in the rest of your landscape with Model Magic trees, flowers, a pond or some animals — whatever you like.

■ Make a long thin snake and wrap it around the edge of your picture for a frame. Let dry at least 24 hours.

■ Glue a picture hanger to the back of your picture. Let dry completely before hanging on a wall.

The Model Magic gifts on this page were made by Andrew, Angel, Christina, Dianna, Desmond, Gaetan, Jason C., Jason W., Kathleen, Kathryn, Kenny, Kenix, Meagan, Rachel, Sandy, Sarah, Sean, Shara, Stephanie, Ryan, and Victor of Christ the King School in Richmond Hill, Ontario.